72016625

J                                          4-6
Monj   Monjo, F.N.
            Slater's mill
4.95

| | | DATE DUE | |
|---|---|---|---|
| | | | |
| | | | |
| | | | |
| | | | |
| | | | |
| | | | |
| | | | |
| | | | |
| | | | |
| | | | |
| | | | |

**DEPARTMENT OF LIBRARIES**
Box 537
Frankfort, Kentucky  40601

# Slater's Mill

# F. N. MONJO

# SLATER'S MILL

ILLUSTRATED BY

## LASZLO KUBINYI

SIMON AND SCHUSTER · NEW YORK

*For my mother*

Text copyright © 1972 by F. N. Monjo
Illustrations copyright © 1972 by Laszlo Kubinyi
All rights reserved
including the right of reproduction
in whole or in part in any form
Published by Simon and Schuster, Children's Book Division
Rockefeller Center, 630 Fifth Avenue
New York, New York 10020

First Printing

SBN 671-65178-1 Reinforced Edition
Library of Congress Catalog Card Number: 73-179990
Designed by Jack Jaget
Manufactured in the United States of America

# Acknowledgments

I should like to express my particular thanks to Nathaniel N. Shipton, manuscript curator of the Rhode Island Historical Society, for supplying me with information concerning Moses Brown; to Richard J. Deeble, president of the Standish-Johnson Outdoor Advertising Company, on India Street, in Providence, who allowed me to see the interiors preserved in his offices, which were originally rooms in the now-demolished Jeremy Sayles (Pidge) tavern; to Paul Rivard, director of the Old Slater Mill Museum, in Pawtucket, who generously supplied me with information concerning Slater and his epoch-making cotton-spinning machines; and to Frank B. Edwards, cotton buyer, of Spartanburg, South Carolina, who gave me the benefit of his many years of experience in the textile industry in his careful reading of the manuscript.

F. N. M.

# Contents

# CHAPTER ONE

# Aboard the New York Packet

The New York packet was nosing its way up the deep blue
stretches of Narragansett Bay.

An hour before, the young Englishman standing at the rail
had seen the town of Newport slide past to starboard. His
companion, the master of the sailing vessel, stamped his feet
on the deck, trying to warm them. It was January, and the
fields and trees slipping past on either side of the bay were
blanketed in snow.

"In a little while now, Mr. Slater," said the captain,
"you'll see the town of Providence. She lies right up at the
head of the bay. On the Seekonk River."

"The Seekonk!" said the young Englishman. "Extraordi-
nary name! Indian, no doubt?"

"Ayeh," said the captain, "Indian. Supposed to mean
somethin' like 'The Haunt of the Wild Goose,' they say. But
the Indians and the wild geese are long gone. Replaced by

shrewd Quaker merchants, and heavy-laden West India-men warped to the docks. It's a mighty busy town."

"I'm anxious to see it," said the young man. "When will we land?"

"Just before lunchtime," said the captain, with a happy sigh. "Packets sailing between New York and Providence can make this journey in eighteen hours, if the wind is right. But when the weather's against us, it may take as much as a whole week."

The vessel creaked and swayed in the morning breeze. The sun sparkled on the waves. Yesterday's gray snow clouds which had laid their white blanket over the land had been swept away by the morning wind.

"Tell me, Captain Brown," said Mr. Slater, "are you per-haps kin to the gentleman I am come to meet?"

"Me? Kin to Moses Brown?" laughed the captain. "No, Mr. Slater. No kin whatever, though I wouldn't be ashamed to own it, if it so happened I were. For he's an honest man, with a conscience. And he *heeds* it, what's more."

"I am glad to know it," said Slater, "for if he and I should take a liking to one another, Mr. Moses Brown may offer me employment."

"You could do a heap worse, young fellow," said the captain. "Moses Brown's a God-fearin' man. And a Quaker, too."

"So I might have guessed, by the 'thee's' and 'thou's' in his letter," Slater replied. "In that case, we should get on well together, Moses Brown and I. For I'm a plain, blunt Englishman."

The captain wondered what business might be bringing Slater from New York to Providence to meet the wealthy Quaker merchant. But he was too proud to let his curiosity

be known, and so said nothing. The tall young man who stood beside him, inhaling the cold fresh air of the winter morning, was as ruddy and sturdy as a yeoman farmer.

"Now, just beyond this point of trees, Mr. Slater," said the captain, "you get your first glimpse of the roofs of Providence. See the spires? And all that forest of masted vessels at the wharfs on India Street?"

As Slater stared, the view grew more distinct. He could see the village roofs and the river. Stately houses climbed a hill to the eastward behind the waterfront. A crescent of eighteen or twenty ships lay nodding gently at the docks.

"A bustling town," said Slater.

"Ayeh," said Captain Brown. "A reg'lar hive of trade. You'll see all you want of her inside half an hour," he said, glancing aft, toward the helmsman. "But I must leave you now, Mr. Slater. I must take the helm myself, if we're not to stray from the channel and run the ship aground on the ledges."

Slater smiled. He hadn't been paying a great deal of attention to the captain. He'd been thinking of his long voyage from England, and of the sights he'd seen in London and New York. And he had been wondering if he would be able to recognize Mr. Moses Brown when the packet tied up in Providence and he stepped off the gangplank onto the Indian Street wharf.

He took a deep breath of the crisp January air. The sloop continued to make its leisurely way through the waters of the bay. The sails cracked and boomed as the packet slowly came about onto the opposite tack. Slater felt his hands trembling with excitement. The ship was drawing closer and closer to port, but he was so impatient to get ashore that it seemed to be taking forever.

# CHAPTER TWO

# A Handsome Proposition

Twenty minutes later the packet was warped alongside the pilings of the dock, and the gangplank lowered into place.

Carrying his small cowhide trunk over his left shoulder, Slater was the first man ashore. The dock was crowded with bales and barrels and drays and porters and soberly dressed citizens who had come down to welcome relatives and friends arriving from New York.

Slater moved rapidly through the throng, taking care not to slip on the snow underfoot. A young man seated in a sleigh behind two glossy chestnut mares caught his eye.

"Art thou just off the New York packet, friend?" asked the fellow. "Do I have the honor to address Mr. Samuel Slater? My name's Obadiah Brown. I'm Moses Brown's son."

The young man hopped down from the sleigh and walked toward Slater to shake hands.

"I'm Samuel Slater," he replied, in his broad Derbyshire

accent. He returned Obadiah's welcoming grip. "I'm come to take a look at your father's cotton-spinning machinery."

"Yes," said Obadiah, "up at the mill, in Pawtucket. Father's told me about thee. He wanted to be here to welcome thee himself, but instead he's up there, on top of the hill, having words with the Colossus of Providence."

"And who might the Colossus of Providence be?" asked Slater, placing his trunk in the sleigh and climbing in beside Obadiah.

"Giddap, Sally! Hup, Sue!" called Obadiah, as he whipped up the chestnut mares. He turned the sleigh around, leaving the waterfront behind them and heading toward the hill on which the largest houses in Providence were situated.

"The Colossus of Providence," said Obadiah, "is what they call my uncle John Brown. He lives in the finest house on Benefit Street, way up there on top of the hill. Father says Uncle John's much too busy storin' up worldly goods here below to pay sufficient mind to charity and other such heavenly treasures, which might profit him more in the world to come. Say! Didst thou take thy lunch aboard the packet? Or has the captain allowed thee to go fasting, Friend Slater?"

"We . . . we docked before luncheon could be served," said Slater.

"Aye," said Obadiah, with a grin. "The captain is known to be anything but open-handed. Much like the Colossus himself!"

The mares had reached the top of the hill, and the sleigh turned off Benefit Street and pulled up in front of a stately brick mansion surrounded by snowy lawns and trees.

"Let me fetch Father," said Obadiah, as he began to

climb the porch stairs. "Wait thee here, Friend Slater, until I tell him thou art come. It's best that I do not ask thee into my uncle's house . . ."

Obadiah broke off as the black face and powdered wig of a butler appeared in the open door. The servant bowed. Obadiah went inside, and the door closed behind him.

The Colossus of Providence must surely be a man of ample means, thought Samuel Slater. He was quite certain that he would not mind being a man of means himself. After all, that was why he had sailed to America in the first place. He wondered if people here would ever call *him* a colossus when he grew rich. Colossus indeed!

The horses, Sally and Sue, stamped in the snow, and drops of water fell from the melting snow in the branches of the larch trees. Far inside the huge brick house, Slater heard the distant thud of a slamming door. Moments later, Obadiah Brown came down the front steps, followed by a spry old fellow dressed in dark brown woolens.

"Father," said Obadiah, "may I present Mr. Samuel Slater. Mr. Slater, Mr. Moses Brown."

"How glad I am to greet thee here at last, Friend Slater," said Moses Brown. "Obadiah tells me that thou hast had a speedy voyage from New York, although thou art famished for food. Were my brother and I on better terms at present, I should invite thee in for some refreshment. But as matters stand, we had best drive thee to Jeremy Sayles's tavern and let him grill us some toasted cheese, with a mug of ale."

"I should be much obliged, sir," said Samuel Slater. "The cold air has given an edge to my appetite."

"That, and thy youth, Friend Slater!" said Moses Brown. "There is nothing whets an appetite so shrewdly as youth! Ah, Obadiah, it is well, it is *well* that I am no longer a business partner of thine Uncle John. He is willful enough to try the patience of an entire choir of angels! He must, at present, be involved in no fewer than *four* lawsuits, simultaneously! And today, he would berate me for opposing ratification of the Constitution! As if his expostulations could ever serve to alter my persuasions! He railed a good two hours at me, whilst I was able to remonstrate but once, saying, 'John Brown, John Brown, thou hast an ungodly temper!' "

"How is that, sir?" said Samuel Slater. "Do I understand, then, that Rhode Island has not yet ratified the Constitution? Is it not a part of the United States? And if it is not, what may it be?"

"At this moment, sir," said Moses Brown, "on this seventeenth day of January, in the year of our Lord one thousand seven hundred and ninety, the little state of Rhode Island and Providence Plantations—the smallest of the original thirteen colonies—stands, alone and undaunted, *outside* the federal union. We are a wholly independent and sovereign state, surrounded by a vast and erring nation—a nation of twelve united but mistaken states—whose new Constitution protects and sanctions black slavery!"

"So that's it," said Slater.

"And Rhode Island shall *never* have my vote for ratification," said Moses Brown, "until the slave trade *and* slavery itself have come to an end throughout the United States. This boy was only two years old," said Moses Brown, gesturing toward Obadiah, "when his mother—she was of the Society of Friends—was taken from us. Anna, my wife, that noble woman, died on February fifth, in 'seventy-three. Before the Revolution began. And a few months after she was gone, I myself joined the Society of Friends. Soon, I too commenced to hate black slavery with all the fervor that

that Society has always brought to bear against it. And then and there I made my will, setting all ten of my slaves free after my death. And twelve or fourteen years after that, when I was in the legislature, I had the satisfaction of seeing Rhode Island outlaw the slave trade. That was just three years ago, in seventeen eighty-seven. And that will explain to thee why I cannot vote today for a Constitution that upholds slavery. Though I *do* honor Mr. Washington, and wish he might be Rhode Island's president too."

"While your brother John . . ." said Slater.

"My brother John, Friend Slater," said Moses Brown, "does not have the tenderest of natures. He gave up the slave trade himself only two or three years ago, when he *had* to, after Rhode Island outlawed it. And the very same year he saw he could no longer legally trade in Guinea, in black human misery, the Colossus turned his eyes to the Orient. Indeed yes. He sent out the first ship ever to sail in the China trade from Providence, the Colossus did. You must have seen her, tied up at the India Street wharf. She's the *General Washington*, and she's back from Madras and Canton, laden down with silk and tea and cloves. But that's John for thee! Forced to give up the Guinea trade, he pushes into something better!

"Well," Moses Brown continued, "my father was known to do some slavin', and I done some myself, twenty, twenty-five years ago. But when all of us shook ourselves free from Britain—after the Revolution, and after I lost my Anna—makin' money out of slavin' was more than I could stomach. I figured good fortune had set *me* free, and others deserved their freedom too. But not John Brown, the Colossus of Providence. He figured . . ."

"Now, Father," said Obadiah, "Mr. Slater didn't come all

17

the way from New York to talk politics."

"True enough," said Moses Brown. "He come on business. Though the goodness knows business and politics are both of them mixed up together, often as not."

"How do you mean, sir?" asked Samuel Slater.

"Well, we Rhode Islanders don't have much farmland, so we have to scratch for a living. Carrying trade, mostly. My father traded to the West Indies in his ship, the *Four Bachelors*. And when Britain tried to put high duties on the molasses we were shipping up here, trade and politics come together with a smash. And right now, today, there's plenty in Rhode Island think that soon's we were to enter the federal union, we'd find our imports taxed to death. So we'll stay *out* of the union! I'm for *free* men and *free* trade, Friend Slater."

"So am I, Mr. Brown," said Slater, "even though I was not born a Yankee."

"It would hev made thy heart sick, Friend Slater, Englishman though thou art, to see what happened to our New England commerce during the war. Why, back in 'sixty-five, my brothers and I had a flourishing business going, manufacturing spermaceti candles. From whale oil, as thou must know. Every month or so, another brother of mine, Nicholas, would have me sail out to Nantucket Island—I'd stay with Nantucket whalers, like Sylvanus Hussey, or Heziah Coffin, or Benjamin Tupper—to buy another cargo of whale oil. Every one of them Quaker captains was making a fortune whaling. And we was doing fine, too, selling candles. But when the war come, the British frigates choked off all shipping, confiscated cargoes, burned our vessels, and left our commerce so badly wrecked it's only in the last five years or so it's come to life again."

"All the towns I've seen since I landed in America, this past November, seem prosperous indeed, Mr. Brown," said Slater.

"So they be," said Moses Brown. "But here we are at the tavern. Obadiah can see to the horses while we go in by the fire and order up some chops and toasted cheese."

Soon the three men were comfortably seated in the tavern's barroom. A huge oaken beam, called the "summertree," ran the width of the room, supporting the ceiling. A large orange fire crackled on the hearth. Moses Brown pointed out the huge butternut tree under which Lafayette had rested when he had had his headquarters in Providence. Lafayette and his troops had come to Rhode Island from France, he explained, to aid the Americans fighting the Revolution.

"Even though Rhode Island is not in the federal union, I see you are an ardent American patriot nonetheless," said Slater.

"Obadiah and I," said Moses Brown, "are members of the Society of Friends, which means we cannot resort to the sword. So I did not take up arms in the struggle, and I remained neutral, as did the rest of the Friends, here and elsewhere. But," he continued with a sly smile, "I will admit to having had something *more* than neutral feelings when I heard the news of the surrender at Yorktown!"

The three men sat eating and drinking before the comfortable fire. Moses Brown told Slater a bit about the faulty cotton-spinning machinery he had bought. He was trying to have it put in proper working order in his factory on the Blackstone River, several miles farther north, in Pawtucket.

"Will I be able to see the machines today?" asked Slater. "Or will it take us the rest of the day to drive there?"

"Nay, nay, Friend Slater," replied Moses Brown, "from Providence to Pawtucket is no long drive. The days are short in January, to be sure, but thou shalt be able to examine my machines early this afternoon, while there is still plenty of daylight left. That I can promise thee."

"Nevertheless, Father," said Obadiah, "we had best pay our host and be on our way."

And the three of them accordingly drank the last of their ale, wrapped themselves up, and called for their sleigh to be brought.

Soon they were speeding over the snowy road, pulled along briskly by the two chestnut mares. Slater drew the bearskin lap robe closer about his knees.

"And am I to suppose, sir," asked Samuel Slater, "that there is plenty of waterpower for the mill wheel? The river —the Blackstone, is it?—plunges over a steep falls at Pawtucket?"

"Thou hast an excellent memory for names, Friend Slater," said Moses Brown. "I hope it may prove as good a memory for the shapes of ratchets and cogs and gears as well." His straight white hair was blown back against the round brim of his Quaker hat. His blue eyes sparkled as brightly as the cold, clear afternoon sky. "The Blackstone River ain't what's at fault, I can tell thee. It pours foaming and frothing over the falls. And the mill wheel creaks and turns as it always hez. Just as it did before I rented the mill from Ezekiel Carpenter."

"And what kind of work, may I ask, sir," inquired Samuel Slater, smiling at the old gentleman, "was Mr. Carpenter doing there?"

"Finishing cloth. Wool. He had a fulling mill out back

where the oil was removed from the wool, and up front, facing the street, he ran a clothing shop, to sell the goods he finished. But no matter. He took all the power he needed, and to spare, from the river."

"And yet the river will not turn your new cotton-spinning machinery, if I understand you?"

Obadiah gave the reins a snap that sent Sally and Sue's hooves clicking over the icy ruts. A tiny chip of ice thrown up from the road stung Slater's lip. He could see the sunlight glinting on the horses' spiked winter shoes.

"The machinery *turns*, all right," said Moses, patiently. "But if we try to run it fast enough to twist a moderate-hard warping yarn, the threads break, and we lose all our time tyin' the loose ends up and startin' in again. If we run any slower, the yarn's too soft and uneven to use for the warp. It's only good for filler. And if we try to turn the machinery by *hand*, the gears are too tiresome to move for long. Oh, we stand in need of expert advice, Friend Slater, I can tell thee! And it's expert advice I hope to hev from thee!"

"It is modern *British* advice," said Samuel Slater. "And I hope it may be expert."

"Well, if it *must* be British, it must! Thou hast said thou wast born in Derbyshire . . ."

"In Belper," said Samuel Slater, with a nod.

"And apprenticed to a partner of the great Sir Richard Arkwright . . ." added Obadiah.

"At the age of fifteen," said Slater.

"By thy looks, thou art no more than sixteen now, lad," said Moses Brown.

"Oh, Mr. Brown," laughed Slater. "I am twenty-two and my papers can prove it. Here, examine my indenture, if you please. It was the only thing in the way of credentials I dared try to smuggle out of England with me, except for what I carried off in my head!"

"Ayeh," said Moses Brown, with a searching look at the young man's forehead. He motioned to Obadiah to pull the sleigh to a halt under an oak tree ridged white with traceries of snow. The flanks of the chestnut mares glistened and steamed in the cold air.

Slater pulled a paper out of his wallet and handed it to the old Quaker.

" 'This indenture witnesseth,' " Moses Brown began, " 'that Samuel Slater of Belper in the County of Derby doth put himself Apprentice to Jedediah Strutt of New Mill in the Parish of Duffield, in the said County of Derby, Cotton Spinner, to learn his art and with him (after the Manner of an Apprentice) to serve from the day of the date of these presents—January eighth, seventeen eighty-three— until the full End and Term of Six Years and an half from thence . . .' "

"Which means," said Samuel Slater, "that as an apprentice I learned the shape and use and function of every single roller and spindle and bobbin in Arkwright's water-spinning frame—the machinery that turns raw cotton into yarn. And when I was seventeen, Mr. Strutt made me overseer of the factory . . ."

"Which *means*," said Moses Brown, staring hard at the indenture, folding it up, and handing it back to Slater, "that thou hast five years' managing experience, and that since July eighth, seventeen eighty-nine, thou hast been a free man."

"Yes. For the past six months," said Slater.

A drop of melting snow fell from the oak tree and landed on the sleeve of his coat.

"Then thou hast chosen the right time to leave England and come to a free country and a new world, young Friend Slater," said Moses Brown, as Obadiah whipped up the mares. "We Yankees concluded our apprenticeship to Britain back in 'eighty-three—just as you began *yours* with Mr. Strutt—and George Washington has now held office for precisely—let me see—eight and one-half months. Ayeh, Mr. Washington was inaugurated in New York City, on April thirtieth, last spring. And he took pains to be wearing a fine, brown suit made of cloth woven in Hartford, Connecticut, I may tell thee."

"Did he indeed, sir?" asked Samuel Slater.

"Good, brown American cloth, it was. But it was *not* woven from yarn that had been spun from start to finish by waterpower, on an Arkwright frame, as thou canst guess. For try as we may to find him, advertise for him and offer prize money as we hev, there is nobody to be found in America who can yet tell us precisely *how* those machines are to be built. Nobody, Friend Slater, unless thou art he!"

Samuel Slater pulled the bearskin tightly about his knees and put his gloved hands back under the robe.

"I have every hope that I may be your man," said Samuel Slater. "I left England with that in mind. I told my mother, my brothers and sisters, nothing of my plans. It was a promise to myself alone."

"Tell me more of what thou hast promised thyself, Friend Slater," said Moses Brown.

"Well, sir, I have promised to make me a rich man. In England, the trade secrets are out. Sir Richard Arkwright lost his patents on the water frames—on the carding and spinning machines—some five or ten years ago."

"That we know," said Moses Brown. "Though precious

24

little good it does *us*, here in America. Your King George is still so jealous of these marvelous engines that he will not let us buy them. When we try to smuggle them out, stripped down, falsely marked, and cunningly crated, his officials break open the boxes and smash the spindles and gears. Nor may we see models of the machines, nor buy plans, so valuable the King believes them to be for assuring England a monopoly on high-quality yarn and cloth."

"And yet at home," said Slater, "back in Lancashire and Nottinghamshire and Derbyshire, the secrets for making Sir Richard Arkwright's machines have been passed from hand to hand. Anyone with capital may now set up a water frame. Why, there are more than one hundred and forty mills in the Midlands today. They click and rattle and whir and spin —profitably, too, I assure you. More are going up every day —some of them powered by *steam*! Mr. Strutt, my old master, told me that there remained plenty of incentive for a young man to set up yet another mill on the River Derwent, in Derbyshire. And so there may be at present—but soon, I think, the spinning business may be overdone in England. So it was for that reason I promised myself that I would become a rich *American*. And so I may, if I prove to be the first man on this side of the Atlantic to build a perpetual spinning frame."

"Thou mayest well be able to keep that promise to thyself, Friend Slater," said Moses Brown, looking shrewdly at the young man. "If, having had oversight of the Arkwright machines, thou canst set my cantankerous machines to running proper yonder in Pawtucket, Rhode Island, *I* can make thee a rich man myself!"

"How rich a man, Mr. Brown?" asked Samuel Slater. "Sir Richard Arkwright used to say that he was making so much money in his mills that—if they'd give him enough time—he could personally pay off the entire national debt!"

Obadiah laughed. Moses Brown lifted his round hat and scratched his white mane. Then he laughed too.

"Friend Slater," he said, "I'm talking 'bout a handsome proposition. A Yankee-good *business* proposition. I'm talking 'bout half the profits."

Samuel Slater turned his head away and frowned down at the snowy drifts speeding away from under the runners of the sleigh.

"A handsome proposition indeed, Mr. Brown," said Samuel Slater. "Although everything depends on the state of those machines of yours—and on how much I can remember."

"We'll see what we shall see," said Moses Brown with a final shake of his head, as he replaced his hat. Obadiah gave the mares another light flick of his whip. The sleigh moved faster through the snow. And the three men fell silent, having very little more to say to one another until they reached Pawtucket.

# CHAPTER THREE

# Sylvanus Brown of Quaker Lane

Pawtucket lay on the west side of the river. Snow carpeted the roofs of the little village, and the early-afternoon sun etched wiry black shadows of the elm trees on the melting drifts. Moses Brown had Obadiah halt the sleigh on a hillock just outside the town.

"Here we be, Friend Slater," he said. "Not yet three o'clock, I calculate. Thou canst see the mill, there," he added, pointing, "on this side the river, just south of the bridge."

"The fulling mill?" asked Samuel Slater.

"Ayeh, the fulling mill that *was*, where the wool was cleaned. Now rented by the unfortunate firm of Almy and Brown, up until now given over to the ruinously unprofitable spinning of mighty weak and uneven cotton yarn. Will Almy is my son-in-law, married to my Sarah. He and Smith Brown, a young kinsman of mine, are trying to make a go

of the yarn business. Thou shalt meet them both, by and by."

"Then you are not in the business yourself, directly, Mr. Brown?" said Samuel Slater.

"Well, I be, and I be-n't," said Moses Brown, with a sigh. "I don't superintend, but I put up most of the money. Had to mortgage two, three of my farms to raise the ready cash. I thank the good Providence above that my brothers and I —James, Nicholas, Joseph, John, Jedediah, and myself—grew sufficiently well fixed in our ripening years. I'm able to live on treasure laid up twenty, thirty years ago. 'Twas all gained in profitable shipping out of Providence, in candles and in the West India trade. Rum, sugar, molasses, cattle, lumber. I needn't worry thee with the inventory. And now that my brother John, the Colossus, is trying his hand in the Orient, I expect he'll make *another* fortune for himself. But Obadiah and I, and my brother Jed, we believe that there's a world of money to be made in spinning and weaving—*if* a perpetual or continuous process can be set up to cut out pretty near all the hand labor."

"And so you and your brother . . ." said Slater.

"No. Jedediah's down in Philadelphia," said Moses Brown, "advertising, 'long with every other mill owner, for those few, rare hands—like thyself—who can remember just a bit about the spinning machinery they once worked back in England. But can't most of them remember too accurate, seems as though. When workers *do* manage to smuggle themselves out of England—they tell me the King won't let them leave if his port officials suspect they've worked in the spinning and weaving mills—once they git over *here*, they seem to forget everything they ever learned."

"The machines are ingenious, devilish marvels of complication, Mr. Brown," said Samuel Slater.

"So they must be," said Obadiah Brown. "For Uncle Jed and his competitors in Philadelphia have had no success all these past years in finding mechanics to build true Arkwright frames."

"And the money thy aging friend Moses Brown hez sunk in Almy and Brown's mill, right here in Pawtucket," said the old Quaker, "hez resulted in nothing more than a few wheezy contraptions that turn out such poor, soft yarn, and so little of *that*, that the sale of it won't pay for the wages of the mill hands. Oh, I tell thee, Friend Slater, thy arrival shall occasion joy and thanksgiving if thou but prove able to revive and resuscitate that heap of ramshackle machinery!"

"I have always, from a child, been of a mathematical turn of mind, Mr. Brown," said Samuel Slater, gazing down at the mill and the bridge and the ice floes bobbing down the river. "My old schoolmaster, Thomas Jackson, used to tell my father he had never seen anyone who loved decimals and fractions as I did. And love them I *did*. Furthermore, I have a precise and tenacious memory for all manner of fittings, and rollers, and gears, and spindles. So it may be that I *can* mend what needs mending, down there at the mill."

"As the Lord wills, Friend Slater, and amen!" said Moses Brown. The horses began moving down the hill on their way into town. "And now look there! Four houses up from the mill. The house with the red barn. By the well, with the stone coping. That's the home of my good friend Oziel Wilkinson. He and his numerous family belong to the Society of Friends, as I do."

"Quakers," said Samuel Slater.

"Nay, Friend Slater, 'Quaker' is a mocking nickname, full

of malicious satire and cruel sarcasm. The name was put upon us in derision, because we quake and tremble, inwardly, when we think of the righteous wrath of the Lord. But it is the Inner Light, within us, that fears the Lord. Ah, yes. There is a Book within us that is not confined to the English or *any* language. And as we silently and reverently wait for its opening, instantly it will teach us. It is the Book of Conscience, and in fear of it we quake and tremble. And for *that* they mock us as 'Quakers.' "

"I did not mean to mock, sir," said Samuel Slater.

"Nay, I know," said Moses Brown, "but it is rather as *Friends* that we strive to be known."

"Friends, then," said Samuel Slater.

"Oziel Wilkinson," said Moses Brown, "is a fine blacksmith and something of a mechanic as well. Since his is the most comfortable house in town, I have arranged for thee to board with him."

"*Board* with him, Mr. Brown?" asked Samuel Slater. "Can you be certain I shall *need* lodgings in Pawtucket? We have struck no bargain as yet that I am aware of."

"Well said, Friend Slater, and very businesslike, too," laughed Moses Brown. "We have struck no bargain, as thou hast declared. But if so happen thou shouldst agree to undertake these repairs, then let me suggest to thee that thou mightst do worse than to board with the Wilkinsons."

"My thanks for the advice, sir," said Samuel Slater. "And now, can you tell me where we will meet with Mr. Smith Brown, and Mr. William Almy? It is with them that I must have my agreement, in writing, is it not? Is the mill operating at present? Will we find these gentlemen in there, with the machines?"

"There thou wilt find them not today, but tomorrow,

Friend Slater, ready to ask thee a hundred questions," said
Moses Brown. "But I had thought to take thee first to this
cottage here, just down the lane . . ."

"They call it Quaker Lane, hereabouts," whispered Obadiah to Slater, so low that his father could not hear. The two
young men exchanged a grin.

"Here lives my kinsman Sylvanus Brown," said Moses
Brown. "Sylvanus is a Yankee-fine carpenter. The best
around. And he understands these spinning machines far
better than I do. I want thee to talk with him this evening,
Friend Slater, and spend the night here with his family.
And Sylvanus'll tell *me* in the morning what he thinks of thy
skill."

# CHAPTER FOUR

# The Bargain

Samuel Slater was amused by the shrewd trick the old Quaker had played on him. But he soon found that Sylvanus Brown did indeed know something about modern spinning machines. Slater liked the master carpenter, with his frank eyes and his open, honest face.

The two of them sat up late that night—hours after Moses and Obadiah had driven back to Providence—talking about the new English spinning machines: Hargreaves' spinning jenny, which easily did the work it had once taken eight pairs of hands to do; Arkwright's spinning frame, which spun cotton thread hard enough to use for warping; another machine called Crompton's mule; and Cartwright's power loom, run by water or steam.

In the morning, when Moses and Obadiah Brown drove back to Sylvanus' cottage, the master carpenter told them that their Mr. Slater seemed to know everything there was to know about the practical side of the business.

"And he's full of ginger, I can tell you," said Sylvanus Brown. "Won't stop to take no breakfast with me. Wants to git right on over to the mill, to look at those machines."

"Well, Friend Slater," said Moses Brown, smiling broadly, "they can wait until we take a dish of tea."

"Nay, I *cannot rest* until I examine those machines, Mr. Brown," said Samuel Slater, striding briskly from the cottage and hurrying down the path to the mill door. Moses Brown shook his head. Obadiah tied the horses to a post in the dooryard, and the three of them hurried over to join Slater, who stood vigorously hammering at the closed door.

"Open up," called Slater, shouting over the whir and rattle of machinery within. "Let us in, there!"

A sturdy ten-year-old boy, his straight blond hair falling over his brown eyes, opened the door and stared up in surprise at the four men. He smiled at Moses Brown.

"Well, now, Master Wilkinson!" said Moses Brown. "Shake hands with Mr. Samuel Slater, who's come here all the way from Derbyshire, England, to build us a first-rate water frame! Friend Slater, meet Smith Wilkinson. Youngest son of Oziel Wilkinson, the blacksmith, he is, and works here in the mill."

"Hello, boy," said Samuel Slater. "Unless I miss my guess, you work in the carding department. Tending the breaker. Am I right?"

"Right indeed, sir," said Smith Wilkinson. "But how can it be that thou knewest, at once?"

"You're too big for tying threads, and you're too bright for a lint sweeper," said Samuel Slater. "And your hands are perhaps a bit roughened from the cards. So I reckoned you'd be tending the breaker. There's but one jenny operating down here, I see. But it can't have more than twenty-four spindles. And a poor, old-fashioned wheezer of a model it is. Power supplied at the moment by that fellow there, turning the hand crank. What's his name, boy? The water frame don't seem to be working. Why's that? Breaking, finishing, drawing, and roving must all be done upstairs on the second floor, am I right? And the cotton wool comes in by wagon, already washed and seeded, and is hoisted up to the third-floor loft for storage—though it *ought* to come up the river. Why don't it? Well, speak up, boy! Let's have some answers!"

"Aye, sir," said Smith Wilkinson, with a gulp. "I been workin' the breaker in the cardin' department 'bout six months . . ."

"Laying the cotton on by hand—taking up a handful and pulling it apart with both hands, to get the staple of the cotton straight?" said Slater.

Smith Wilkinson nodded, and Moses Brown grinned at Sylvanus and Obadiah.

"Then you fix the handful of cotton," said Slater, "holding it firm, and you lay it on the surface of the breaker, moving your hand back and forth across the card till you see the lap well begun . . ."

"Thou wast once on the breaker thyself, wast thou not?" asked Smith Wilkinson, smiling up at the tall young Englishman.

"Aye, for about six months," said Slater, "until I moved on up to the finisher—which you yourself should soon be doing, I'm thinking. But you haven't answered my questions, boy."

"Thou hast guessed, sir. I'm too big for tyin' threads, so I'm on the breaker. And the wheezin' old jenny has only the

twenty-four spindles, as thou hast seen. And the fellow
turnin' the hand crank is Samuel Brunius Jenks. Come over
here, Sam, and meet Mr. Sam Slater! And he's *got* to turn it
by hand because the water wheel is froze in the ice at the
river's edge. And the big water frame is broke anyway, and
too heavy to turn by hand even if it *was* workin'. And the
cotton comes in by wagon from the village and the farms
round about, where the seeds are picked out by hand, so it
wouldn't save nothin' to be brought upriver noways, 'less
it could come already cleaned. And it's hoisted up to the
third-floor loft, as thou hast said. Then I feed it into the
breaker, where the teeth—the cards—on the rollers scratch
out the leaves and sticks and lay the cotton fibers straight.
And out it comes in a nice, white, fluffy, even blanket of
cotton."

"Called a lap," said Samuel Slater.

"Don't I *know?*" said Smith Wilkinson. "And I carry the
finished lap to the *next* cardin' machine . . ."

"The finisher," said Slater.

"Aye," said Smith Wilkinson, "and it's there that the lap
is fed into the rollers that stretch and comb it some more,
and then narrow the blanket of cotton down to a little band
'bout three inches wide . . ."

"Called . . . ?" asked Slater.

"Called a sliver," said Smith Wilkinson. "And the slivers
finally come out and coil up into a can. And the cans are
carried over to the *next* machine, the drawin' frame. And
when *that's* workin'—which it ain't today—the slivers go
through some more rollers that stretch the cotton fibers out
even further, and then the smaller slivers go through the
reed, which divides and narrows 'em down still more . . ."

"And in a good, new drawing frame, my lad," said Slater,

"we double the sliver back on itself once, for strength, and give it the first twist or two."

"Not here," said Smith Wilkinson, scratching the calf of his left leg with his right foot.

The big Negro who had been turning the crank of the spinning jenny now stood beside the boy.

"Sam Jenks," said Smith Wilkinson, "this is Mr. Samuel Slater, from England. He used to work on the breaker, same as me!"

"Pleased to meet you, Mr. Slater," said the huge fellow, bowing to the Englishman.

"How d'ye do, Sam Jenks," said Samuel Slater, with a brisk nod. "And after the narrowed slivers leave the drawing frame, Master Wilkinson, where do they go next?"

"To the rovin' frame. More rollers. More stretchin'. More narrowin'. And some twistin' as well. Until the rovin's come out, reeled onto bobbins, ready for the spinnin' frame. Then I take the rovin's, reeled up on their bobbins, downstairs. And down here they're put onto the water frame, when *it* ain't broke. And the threads are twisted and twisted on the rollers and spindles, until the finished yarn can be reeled off onto spools—ready for weavin' on the loom with the fly shuttle. But when the water frame's broke, as it is now . . ."

"As it is *mostly*," said Sam Jenks.

". . . then we have to spin the rovin's on the spinnin' jenny, and Sam, here, turns it by hand," said Smith Wilkinson.

"My compliments, Master Wilkinson," said Moses Brown. "Thou hast answered every question put to thee by Friend Slater."

"And with a certain breathless grasp of the business, too, I'll be bound," said Obadiah, with a glance at his father.

"Yes. Yes. He's a quick, bright boy, is Master Smith Wilkinson," said Samuel Slater. "But I must ask one question more."

"Yes, sir?" inquired Smith Wilkinson.

"Where are Mr. William Almy, and Mr. Smith Brown? Mr. Moses Brown has told me I would find them here at the mill."

"They're over to home, with Mother and Father, breakfastin' on hot beef pie," said Smith Wilkinson.

"Well, well," said Moses Brown, "then we must join them."

"Nay, Mr. Brown," said Samuel Slater. "I will see the rest of the machinery first, and inspect the loft, before I take any breakfast."

And Samuel Slater climbed rapidly up the ladder to the second floor. Moses Brown, Smith Wilkinson, Obadiah, and Sylvanus climbed the ladder after him, and stood staring at him in wonderment. Slater darted from the breaker to the finisher to the drawing frame and at last to the roving frame. The handful of children working the machines stared at the Englishman in his overcoat and leather boots. He seemed to understand every comb and roller and flywheel at a glance. He visited the loft for a split second, then climbed down the ladders to the first floor and stood staring at the snow by the front door. He began kicking at a clump of ice adhering to the iron boot scraper.

"Art thou downhearted at what thou hast seen, Friend Slater?" said Moses Brown.

"Aye!" sighed Slater. "These machines will *not do*, Mr. Brown. They are good for *nothing* in their present condition, nor can they be made to answer."

"But I have spent hundreds and hundreds of dollars on

these machines, Mr. Slater! Surely thou canst contrive to repair them!" said Moses Brown.

"I tell you, Mr. Brown, they *cannot* be repaired. They *will not do*! They must be sold off. Discarded. Everything must be rebuilt, from start to finish, from cellar to attic, or I will not so much as put my hand to the business!"

Moses Brown shook his head, and cast his eyes upward in resignation and despair. Then he heard familiar voices, and looked down sharply. Coming up the path were his son-in-law and his kinsman.

"Will Almy! Smith Brown!" he called. "Let me make ye acquainted with our young English mechanic, Mr. Samuel Slater. Mr. Slater it is who can build the Arkwright machinery. But wait! Before ye rejoice, I must tell ye that he hath examined thy machines, and come to a most doleful and a most *expensive* conclusion."

"Well, Mr. Slater?" asked William Almy.

"How much will it cost to repair them?" asked Smith Brown.

"Speak up, man," said Moses Brown.

"Gentlemen," said Samuel Slater, "it is not a question of repairs. These wretched contraptions *cannot* be repaired. I have just now done telling Mr. Moses Brown that they are useless. They will *never* spin strong yarn. I say clear them out, lock, stock, and barrel, and let us begin afresh!"

"Throw out the entire works?" gasped William Almy.

"From the loft to the basement," said Slater, calmly pulling on his gloves. "*Nothing* here will serve. Everything is rickety, antiquated, and has long since been discarded in all our modern British mills. With half the profits as my compensation, I shall build you a new set of excellent machinery. I shall pay the entire cost of these new machines out of

my share if, under my proposals, I do not make you as good yarn in this mill as any that is spun back home in England. If I fail you, I shall have *nothing* for my services, and will throw the whole of what I have attempted over the bridge. But I shall *never* try to repair these wretched, backwoods, Colonial wheezers! Nay, gentlemen. A new set of machinery or nothing. Take it or leave it. What shall it be?"

Moses Brown glanced at young Smith Wilkinson, who stood smiling at Slater.

"It shall be as thou wouldst have it, Mr. Slater," said Moses Brown. "I shall pay for thy new machines."

"On one condition!" said Samuel Slater. "I know the value of the machinery I shall build, and I will *not* have my designs stolen and copied abroad by all and sundry. I shall not build the new machines unless you promise me I can have master mechanics to work with—men I can trust completely —men *sworn* to secrecy! Otherwise we have no bargain here!"

"We have thy men," said Moses Brown. "Sylvanus Brown and Oziel Wilkinson will keep thy secrets to the grave."

"I must tell Father!" cried Smith Wilkinson, with a whoop, as he ran to tell the good news.

"Then let us shake hands upon our bargain," said Samuel Slater, pulling off the glove from his right hand. The six men shook hands in the doorway, and Slater carefully replaced his glove.

"And now," said Slater, "I should like a slice of that hot beef pie, if Mrs. Wilkinson will oblige me. And then I must have a long talk with my master mechanic and blacksmith, Mr. Oziel Wilkinson. In private!"

# CHAPTER FIVE

# The Breaker

In the months that followed his January sleigh ride to Pawtucket, Samuel Slater found that he was often working sixteen hours a day, six days a week. Even on the Sabbath, when the mill was shut down, his mind was on his machines.

He followed Moses Brown's advice and rented a room in Oziel Wilkinson's house, and he took his meals at Mrs. Lydia Wilkinson's bountiful table. Mrs. Wilkinson was a good cook and always made sure that the slim young Englishman was served with a heaping plenty of roast, gravy, biscuits, dumplings, and bacon. She piled his plate higher than she did those of her own sturdy sons. The two older Wilkinson boys, David and Abraham, were blacksmiths, like their father.

The Wilkinson girls, Sarah and Hannah, dressed much alike in plain gray wool dresses and white Quaker caps. They were both shy with Samuel, but it was Hannah who smiled at him first. And it was Hannah to whom he talked most often of his boyhood home in Belper.

During January and February, Sam Jenks and the Wilkinson men helped Slater dismantle the old cotton-spinning machinery. Once it was removed, the empty mill echoed hollowly under their footsteps. To hide from curious townspeople the new machinery he would soon be building, Slater covered the first-floor windows of Sylvanus Brown's cottage with heavy shutters.

In March, Sylvanus began helping him with his work. After making him promise he would never give away the secrets about to be passed on to him, Slater took a piece of chalk and began marking on an oaken plank. He drew the outline of one of the spindles he'd need for the new spinning frame. Sylvanus Brown sawed it out and put it on the lathe, where he turned and shaped it and bored through its length exactly as Slater wished. As each part was completed, Slater chalked out another, and Sylvanus turned and finished it on the lathe.

Oziel Wilkinson and his two older sons were busy in their blacksmith shop, shaping fittings and rollers and gears and shafts for the carding machines and for the drawing and roving frames.

"I'll need still another blacksmith if I'm to get my breaker and finisher built this year," said Samuel Slater.

"Well, sir," replied Smith Wilkinson, "when Father has more work than he can handle, he sometimes gives some out to Mr. Pliny Earl. Wouldst thou want me to ask him if he can give us a hand?"

"Yes, ask him, boy," said Slater. And so Pliny Earl was soon at work making the thousands of tiny metal teeth that were set in leather and then wrapped tightly around the re-

volving drums and fastened to the fixed cards on the carding machine.

"No yarn mill is any better than its carding machines,"
Slater observed darkly to Sam Jenks and Smith Wilkinson.

It was now late in April, and they were down at the river-
side, repairing some broken paddles in the mill wheel. The
rushing water roared steadily over the falls.

"The carders are the machines that take up the raw cotton, first off, and if they don't comb and card the staple
straight, and lay the fibers out long and even as can be, no
amount of stretching and twisting and spinning later on can
turn out a fine, hard yarn," said Slater. "And if it turns out
too soft, and breaks easily, then it's not strong enough to be
used for warp thread, for the warp threads have much more
strain on them than the woof does, when they're in the
loom."

"It's a wonderment to me, Mr. Samuel," said Sam Jenks,
"you can keep all these machinery plans inside your head,
like you do. And keep 'em all sorted out, too."

"It's a greater wonderment to *me*, Sam," said Slater, "that
anyone could ever have been shrewd enough to invent them
in the first place. I'm only copying their work, you know, or
*trying* to. Every fellow among them must have been ten
times smarter than I am. And plenty of them got small
thanks for their pains, too."

"Was there such a crowd of fellows, then, Mr. Slater?"
asked Smith Wilkinson. "I thought it was nobody but Arkwright invented the water frame, and all the other claptrap
goes with it."

"Far from it, young Master Wilkinson," said Samuel
Slater. "There were many, many inventions ahead of Arkwright's. It all began thirty, forty years before I was born,
when John Kay . . ."

"Another Britisher?" asked Smith Wilkinson.

"Yes, my lad," laughed Slater. "He and most of the other inventors I'm talking about happened to be Britishers. But there'll still be plenty of room for smart young Yankees like you. John Kay put the first fly shuttle on the old hand loom. Before that, the weavers had had to throw the shuttle back and forth across the taut threads—across the warp—by hand. Kay's invention snapped *two* shuttles back and forth, worked by springs, so the weaving could be turned out much faster—more than *twice* as fast. And after that came Lewis Paul and John Wyatt, who learned they could use rollers to spin thread faster than it could be spun one thread at a time, by hand, on a spinning wheel. And just a year or so before I was born, a little girl about four years old, named Jenny Hargreaves, happened to knock over the spinning wheel in her family's cottage—in Blackburn, over in Lancashire, about sixty miles from where I was born. When Jenny's father, James Hargreaves, saw that the spindle and the wheel kept on whirling, even when the whole contraption lay on its side, the thought came to him that six or eight spindles might be turning there just as easy as *one*. So he geared up eight spindles to a single wheel, and he saw he could spin *eight times as much* thread as he used to spin with a single pair of hands. And when he'd improved his machine and patented it, he called it the spinning jenny, after his little girl."

"Well, I never did know about little Jenny," said Sam Jenks, "and I been turning that creaky old spinnin' jenny in the mill for a good long time."

"And you want to know what the neighbors *did* to his machine, in Blackburn, when they found out what it could do?" asked Samuel Slater.

"They try to copy it?" said Smith Wilkinson.

"They did not," said Samuel Slater. "They broke into his cottage and smashed it up! They were mostly all spinners themselves, you see, and they were afraid a machine like that—like the spinning jenny—would put most of them out of work. They would have killed Hargreaves, maybe, if they could have found him. But he slipped away to Nottingham and kept safe. He never did get rich, though. But Arkwright did, improving two or three ideas that other men had had, for spinning by means of rollers. He set up mills that were run throughout by waterpower, where the raw cotton came in at one end, in pods and baskets, and came out the other spun onto bobbins, all ready for weaving on the loom. And his machines spun cotton yarn so hard you could use it for warp thread—*lots* cheaper than the linen thread they'd had to use before—and so *his* cloth was all cotton, and dirt cheap. That's why he's one of the richest men in England today, though he can scarcely read and write. Arkwright was too poor to go to school when he was a boy, and started out apprenticed to a barber. Now he's been knighted by the King for inventing his 'claptrap,' as you call it."

"And all his money came out of the spinnin' frame?" asked Smith Wilkinson.

"Every penny," said Samuel Slater. "Barrels of money. Streams of money. One long continuous trickle of cotton, humming and twisting and spinning itself into an endless river of gold . . ."

"Maybe we all get rich too, Mr. Slater," laughed Sam Jenks.

"Maybe we will," said Samuel Slater. "There's hundreds of mill owners getting richer by the minute in the English Midlands, while we sit talking. And they're improving their machines all the time. Sam Crompton took the best features of the spinning jenny and put them together with Arkwright's water frame. And because he crossed the breed—as you might cross a mare and a jackass—they named it Crompton's 'mule.' *That* came along when I was a lad, eleven or twelve. When I was just about your age, Master Wilkinson," said Samuel Slater. "And just a year or two ago," he continued, "a minister of the Church of England—a *parson*, mind you—invented the power loom. The Reverend Edmund Cartwright, from Nottingham. A loom turned by a water wheel, or a steam engine, clattering out yard after yard of linens or broadcloth. An invention making possible untold thousands of bolts of finished goods—machine-made throughout. 'Claptrap,' Master Wilkinson? Oh, no. There's *fortunes* to be made in mills and machines, I can tell you. And not a moment to spare, if we're to get our share!"

Samuel Slater threw down his hammer and ran up the steps to the mill.

"All business, ain't he?" said Smith Wilkinson, as he turned back to the water wheel.

"Mighty full of perseverance, and a plenty spit and vinegar besides," said Sam Jenks. "Anyone get this mill turnin', *he* will."

But Slater had begun to doubt if he could do the job at all. More than three months had passed since Moses Brown's sleigh had delivered him to the mill. He had very little to show for all the money he had spent on tools and machinery. And little to show for his time.

He had received a letter from Moses Brown the week before, written from Providence. "Write me any good news thou canst honestly send me, Friend Slater," the old Quaker had written, "for truly, I may tell thee, I grow discouraged with the slow progress of thy work, and alarmed by the great cost of thy machines. I had thought $300 would have repaired the old works, but thou has spent four times that sum to date, and as yet there is not one single spindle turning . . ."

It was true. Only one of the two new spinning frames was even close to being finished. As Slater walked into the mill, he saw Oziel and David Wilkinson adjusting one of the fluted rollers, explaining the workings of its twenty-four spindles to Torpen and Eunise Arnold. The Irish couple and their children, Charles and Annie Arnold, had worked the old frame before it broke down. They had promised Slater that they would tend the new one, "oncet it was workin'." But when would that be?

Slater was so busy with his machines that he paid very little attention to the momentous news, in May, that Rhode Island had at last voted to ratify the Constitution of the United States. Moses Brown had not voted in its favor, he knew. But Slater had heard that the U. S. Senate had threatened to deal with Rhode Island as if she were a foreign nation, placing import duties on her products, if she remained aloof from the rest of the states any longer. So the little state rapidly chose to join the Union, and celebrated her changed estate with booming cannon and bonfires.

Slater was far more concerned with the bad news that it would take more than another three months to complete the larger, forty-eight-spindle frame that must be built next. Moses Brown would never stand for the expense! To be sure, Slater had a signed agreement in his wallet, witnessed by Oziel and Abraham Wilkinson, setting up the new firm of Almy, Brown & Slater. The paper was all signed and legal. But it provided that he, Samuel Slater, was to pay half the cost of the machines, the money to be deducted from *his* half of the profits of the sale of yarn turned out by the mill. And until the machines began spinning, there could be no yarn to sell, and no profits. That meant that there was no one to put up the money meanwhile, except Moses Brown. And Slater could not expect canny old Moses Brown to go on forever mortgaging more and more of his farmlands in order to raise money for the mill.

If I can't show them that I can get these frames built, as I promised, thought Slater, he'll decide I must be an impostor. A fraud! He'll refuse to throw good money after bad. And my main chance will be lost. All my hopes will come wheezing to a dead halt, like those rickety old machines they had here back in January.

He waved glumly to the group clustered about the spinning frame. Then he climbed the ladder to the second floor. There he saw the awkward, mysterious shapes of four partially completed machines. The drawing frame and the roving frame, at the far end of the room, and the finisher, nearby, were all deserted. But there was a small knot of faces surrounding the breaker. Pliny Earl and Sylvanus Brown were bent over the half-completed machine, showing three boys how to fasten the rows of steel teeth, or cards, set in leather, to the surface of the main cylinder. The two black faces belonged to Johnny and Varnus Jenks, Sam's sons. The third boy, working with pliers and an awl, was Otis Borrows.

"Thought I'd lend you a hand, Pliny," said Slater. "I can't wait to see this devil put together proper, and starting to turn out some decent work."

"Got the boys workin' for us," grinned Pliny Earl. "No

reason they shouldn't know somethin' 'bout all these cylinders of Satan, since they goin' to hev to learn to dodge 'em later on, soon's they start gyratin' and revolvin'."

"And I hope that's going to be mighty soon," said Samuel Slater.

"No, sir, Mr. Slater," said Varnus Jenks. "Mr. Sylvanus Brown say we got another two, three weeks on this one 'fore we be through."

"That right, Sylvanus?" said Slater. "Bad as all that?"

"Well, there ain't no parts to be had, ready-made, Mr. Slater," said Sylvanus Brown, in his slow Yankee manner. "Ever' one of these thousands of blessed teeth got to be set by hand, by Pliny and me, don't they? Same for the rollers and the gears and the levers. Wilkinson's got to make ever' one of them special, to order, on his forge. Why, we even hev to try to whack up most of our own machine tools. They don't hev *half* of what-all we need, down Providence. Nor nowhere's else. You understand what I'm sayin', Mr. Slater?"

"I understand, Sylvanus," sighed Slater. "I understand all too well. But let us do what we can. Hand me that extra awl, Otis Borrows. Johnny Jenks, did anyone ever explain to you and Otis and Varnus just how this breaker's meant to work? Speak up!"

"Cotton first comes in on the rollers, and they mash it down, kind of," said Johnny.

"And what are them rollers called, boy? What did I tell you?" prompted Pliny Earl.

"Them rollers the *urchins*," said Varnus Jenks.

"That's right. Urchins," said Samuel Slater. "Then what happens?"

"Urchins put the cotton on the main cylinder," said Varnus, "and it goes 'round that, till it comes to this second smaller cylinder . . ."

"No," said Slater. "Not yet. Over the top of the main cylinder there'll be ten sets of fixed teeth, or cards, that comb the cotton as it turns and moves up around the main cylinder. Then, as the cotton comes on around and down, still on the big cylinder, it's taken off onto the smaller cylinder."

"That's right. That's the doffin' cylinder," said Otis Borrows. "The one with the cards set 'round in spiral pattern. And it turns in the opposite direction from the main cylinder."

"And the cotton fibers get combed again as they go 'round on the doffin' cylinder," said Johnny Jenks.

"And how's it all lifted off?" asked Slater. "That's the most interesting, the most beautiful operation in the whole process. Pliny? Sylvanus? Well, look here. This metal plate —later on it will be set with teeth all along the edge, like a comb—this plate moves rapidly up and down. It works by a crank, and it moves up and down, up and down. Each time it rises it lifts part of the cotton fleece—the even blanket of cotton that's now called the lap—up off the teeth of the doffing cylinder, and passes that lap of cotton through two more rollers, *smooth* rollers, and right off the machine! Wait till you see it working, boys! It's beautiful!"

"Well, sir," said Pliny Earl, "it's a long way from workin', yet. And be a sight *more* time and money poured into this devilish whirligig 'fore we be done!"

Slater said nothing to Pliny Earl in reply. He knew the man was right. The work was going slowly, even though he and Sylvanus and Pliny and the Wilkinsons often found themselves sweating over their machines from five in the morning until eight or nine at night.

May, June, and July slipped away. In August, President Washington and Secretary of State Thomas Jefferson sailed up to Providence from New York to pay their compliments to the new state of Rhode Island. There were more salvos of cannon and more bonfires, but Slater was too busy with his machines to attend the celebrations.

Now both water frames—the twenty-four-spindle and the forty-eight-spindle machines—stood ready. And the drawing frame and the roving frame were nearly ready, too. The attic loft was bulging with raw cotton. Even the water wheel itself had been fitted with a new axle of elmwood and a new set of maplewood paddles, ready to start turning as soon as the sluice gate was opened and the water from the Blackstone River was allowed to rush into the race. But no cotton could be spun into yarn until both the breaker and the finisher, in the carding department, were in perfect working order.

The men were so busy with their machines that the making of a perfect new gear in the smithy was a matter of much greater moment than the news, in September, that President Washington and the rest of the federal government were about to move the capital from New York to Philadelphia.

Completing the finisher required all their attention. It was October before Slater said it would do. Moses Brown, Smith Brown, and William Almy continued to complain, in person and by letter, of the long delays and the terrible costs. "Thou must be acutely sensible, Friend Slater," wrote Moses Brown, at the beginning of November, "that before another ten or twelve weeks have passed away, thou wilt have consumed a *full year* in building thy cards and combs and cranks and frames and jennies, with not so much as a single yard of spun yarn to give hope or satisfaction unto thee and thy pursuits, or unto thy steadfast, patient friend and humble servant, Moses Brown."

How much longer could that patience last? Everything depended on the final link in the chain—the breaker. Slater had tried to recall every detail of the carding machines he had operated and supervised for so many years at Jed Strutt's New Mill, in Duffield. But sometimes the young Englishman would wake in the night with a start, having dreamed that he had forgotten the proper shape of an intricate cog or gear. The breaker would shriek out a creaking warning and the rollers would jam and the cotton would foam upward, like white rapids in an angry stream, spilling off the rollers onto the factory floor.

On one such night, Hannah Wilkinson woke up when she heard Slater cry out, "I must remember! I *must remember!*" But after she opened his bedroom door, she saw that he was only tossing and murmuring in his sleep. She closed the door softly, and decided that she must say nothing to anyone about his nightmare.

He had been much too busy to talk with her often, for he rose at sunup, and usually went back to the mill after supper, to work by lantern light. But there were Sundays, when all work must stop, in observance of the Sabbath.

Slater had heard several jocund fellows in Pawtucket joke about the long, sometimes utterly silent Quakers meetings, where the Friends sat side by side, in quiet rows, waiting for the Inner Light of conscience to bid one of them speak out. There was no minister to deliver a sermon: any inspired man or woman in the congregation was free to testify, or pray, or preach, or exhort.

Slater grew to admire the Quakers for their charity, their sobriety, and their hatred of oaths and violence and warfare. Living with the Wilkinsons, he learned that Quakers would never swear an oath of any kind—not even an oath taken on the Bible, in court—which kept most of them out of litigation and out of all political office. For instead of *swearing* to tell the truth, a Quaker would merely permit himself to *affirm* his willingness to tell the truth.

Slater also learned that Quakers shunned music and dancing, card playing, gambling, and other pastimes that seemed frivolous to them. But the rule that began to concern Slater most was the Quaker practice of "reading out of the meeting," or expelling from the church body, any member who married someone of another faith.

For on some of those Sunday afternoons during the summer and autumn, Hannah and Slater had walked together, while he spoke of his mother and father; of "Holly House," the farm where he had been born; and of his four older brothers. He told Hannah that his father, William, had been a well-to-do farmer and timber merchant, who had allowed his youngest son to be apprenticed to the cotton-spinning trade because his good friend and neighbor Jed Strutt needed a bright lad to help him run things at the mill. Strutt had particularly asked for one of the Slater boys.

"So Father let me go to Mr. Strutt," said Samuel, "though I was the youngest of the five, for he said I had the best head for mathematics among the lot of us, and he thought I had a way with machines."

Hannah Wilkinson was sitting beside him, under a huge walnut tree. Narrow bands of October sunlight slanted through the few remaining leaves. Her bright hair was all but hidden under her starched cap.

55

"Hannah," said Samuel, "if I am able to set the mill in order, and if I ever get things running . . . Hannah. I love you."

Hannah stood up and began walking away. How could she answer? Mother and Father belonged to the Society of Friends. Samuel Slater did not. She could not possibly hope that Father would allow her to marry him. Not *ever*. She must not even ask herself why her eyes were beginning to fill with tears.

Samuel Slater wished he had not spoken his feelings. How could he think of marrying until he had enough money to take care of a wife and family? And how could there ever be money enough until the breaker was built, and the mill humming?

He gave up his Sunday walks with Hannah and spent even more of his time at the mill. November turned to December, and now, on those dark, wintry mornings, he found ice at the river's edge, growing thicker day by day. Whenever he wanted to test his machines, he first had to take an axe and break up the ice imprisoning the mill wheel. The axle was usually tight-frozen, too.

At the end of the first week in December, every single gear and fitting in the breaker had been oiled and polished, ready for the test run. Smith Wilkinson had asked if he might feed the first handfuls of raw cotton onto the belt, and Samuel Slater had smiled and said yes. The entire Wilkinson family climbed the ladder to the second floor of the mill and clustered around the machine. Torpen and Eunise Arnold and their two children, Annie and Charles, ran their fingers over the still rollers, whispering excitedly to each other. Sam Jenks and Varnus and Johnny and Otis

Borrows were there. Sylvanus Brown, the carpenter, and Pliny Earl, the blacksmith, patted the breaker as if it were a temperamental racehorse that had to be soothed.

"She's a beauty," said Abraham Wilkinson, rubbing his hand over the wiry stubble on his jaw.

"A beauty," said Samuel Slater, *"provided* she combs the cotton as she's meant to do. We'll see soon enough. Sam Jenks! Slip that belt onto her flywheel, and we'll give her a try!"

Sam engaged the moving belt that brought power up to the second story from the rotating water wheel. The breaker shuddered, and all her cylinders began to whir and turn. The wooden urchins gleamed and rolled, merrily. The main cylinder, with its thousands and thousands of teeth, glittered wickedly as it began its slow revolution. The doffing cylinder moved obediently in the opposite direction. The metal plate, with its toothed edge, clattered nervously up and down, lifting off an imaginary blanket of cotton from the doffer and passing it on to the final pair of purring rollers.

"It's working, sir!" hollered Smith Wilkinson. "It's working perfect!"

"It's a marvel," said Hannah Wilkinson, looking straight at Samuel Slater.

Smith Wilkinson and Varnus Jenks dragged a hamper of raw cotton over to the breaker belt.

"Ain't you goin' to feed this contraption?" asked Torpen Arnold. "I feel like I been waitin' half my life to see this thing start gobblin' cotton."

"So have I," said Samuel Slater with a sigh, as he adjusted the second urchin roller. "Smith Wilkinson," said he, "you may begin laying on."

"Yes, sir!" hollered Smith Wilkinson. He plunged his left hand into the hamper and fluffed the cotton, pulling it apart with both hands, straightening the staple. He held it firm. Then he laid it on the breaker belt, moving his right hand back and forth, spreading it out evenly. Handful followed handful as he quickly patted the cotton and spread it over the moving belt. A smooth mat of fibers emerged from between the urchin rollers and was scratched up and caught fast by the first band of teeth on the main cylinder. The thin cotton blanket moved slowly forward as the big drum turned. Soon half the cylinder was covered with clinging whiteness. But somewhere within, as the snowy tide began passing the fixed cards on top of the cylinder—where the fibers should have begun to be raked and combed—the breaker began to rattle and shiver. It growled a deep, angry warning, which rose to a treble whine. The gears were straining to move the main cylinder forward. But the cotton was beginning to tangle in the teeth of the fixed combs on top of the drum. Cotton seemed to be piling up in soft, fat clots all around the main cylinder.

"Looks like lumps of clabber," said Lydia Wilkinson, with a sorrowful shake of her head.

"So it does, Mother Wilkinson," said Samuel Slater, flinging his wrench to the floor in despair. "Though it ought to look like a maiden's hair after a brushing—sleek and smooth and silky."

"What's *wrong* with thee, thou cylinder of Satan!" roared Oziel Wilkinson, giving the breaker frame a savage kick.

The machine's angry gears whined louder and louder in high, thin protest as more cotton backed up behind the fixed comb's teeth. The main cylinder slowed almost to a dead halt.

"Cotton's fallin' off the main cylinder. Better stop her quick, or you'll break something sure," said Pliny Earl, looking as if he might begin to cry.

"Yes, stop her," said Slater to Sam Jenks. But even before the big Negro could throw the lever, there came a final growl of rage, the sound of snapping iron, and a thunderous clank.

There was dead silence after the gears stopped straining. Nobody spoke. White and stricken, Samuel Slater stared at the traitorous machine.

"Look at that, sir," said Smith Wilkinson, in a frightened whisper. "She went and snapped the gear."

# CHAPTER SIX

# The Teeth of the Main Cylinder

"Thou art downhearted, Samuel," said Mistress Lydia Wilkinson. "Don't let thy courage desert thee, now. Thy race is but begun." She forked a huge chunk of corned beef onto a platter and began surrounding it with mounds of boiled cabbage, parsnips, carrots, onions, turnips, and potatoes. "There's boiled beef tonight. A good, hearty New England boiled dinner. So eat well, for thine own sake, even though thy spirit's troubled, so thou mayest grow pert and strong in no time!"

Sarah and Hannah Wilkinson were setting mugs of cider, pitchers of milk, plates, pies, loaves of bread, and crocks of butter and pickles on the long kitchen table. Smith Wilkinson had been sent down to the forge to tell his father and brothers to wash up and come home for supper.

"I *am* downhearted, Mother Wilkinson," said Samuel Slater. "What do you suppose Moses Brown will say when he hears that my breaker won't comb cotton wool? He'll say I'm a cheat and an impostor. He'll say I never had any oversight of the Arkwright machines in Britain, nor anywhere else. He'll think me a fraud!"

"Oh, no, Samuel. He will not!" said Hannah, banging a stool in place at the table. "He'll think no such thing."

"He knows how good a mechanic thou art," said Sarah.

"And he knoweth a fine young man when he appeareth," said Lydia Wilkinson. "Oziel and I have spoke naught but good of thee to Mr. Moses Brown. Mr. Moses Brown may be a bit near when money is in question, but he is an honest man and a Friend, and he knoweth thee very well for what thou art. Vex not thyself with thoughts of Mr. Moses Brown."

"There were other hopes as well, Mother Wilkinson," said Samuel Slater, "which cannot now be thought of."

Hannah had been leaning over the table, about to set down a glass of jelly. When Samuel spoke, the jelly glass fell from her hand and smashed the pitcher of milk.

"Hannah!" exclaimed Sarah, as her sister turned and ran from the room. "Didst thou see, Mother? Hannah's hands were trembling, and her cheeks were red!"

"We all be troubled for Samuel's sake tonight, Sarah," said Lydia Wilkinson. "He hath had grave disappointment with the machines today, as all of us have witnessed." She mopped up the milk and threw the broken pitcher into the trash barrel. "And Sister Hannah feeleth that sadness too."

"You'll forgive me, Mother Wilkinson," said Samuel Slater, rising from the bench where he was seated. "But I've no hunger in me tonight. I can't think of anything but that breaker! What *is* it I've forgot? I keep asking myself *where* it was I made my error! I had a dream that this would hap-

pen, you know. And here it's all come to nothing, just as I feared and dreamed it might happen."

"Thou canst not say that all hath come to naught yet, Samuel," said Lydia Wilkinson. "There's many a tomorrow for thee, in which to put all things aright. Thou must take thyself to bed, boy, and dream of happier fortunes. Thine engines await thee, tomorrow, at the mill, and all of us can help thee with another effort."

Samuel Slater smiled at her, and climbed the stairs to his bedroom. He could hear Hannah crying softly in her pillow, in the room across the hall. He heard Oziel Wilkinson and his sturdy sons tramp into the kitchen downstairs, draw their stools up to the table, and begin their supper of corned beef and cabbage.

The night was dark and cloudy. There was no moon. Samuel Slater could hear a hissing and rasping, like sand thrown against the windowpanes. It must be sleet, or snow, he thought. He shivered and pulled the quilt up around his ears. The sleet made a dismal sound that made him think of death. And death made him think of that August afternoon back in '83, when he was just fifteen and had been apprenticed to Jedediah Strutt for little more than half a year. His brother William had ridden over to Duffield, where Samuel was working on the breaker, laying-on. And William came into the mill and stood by the machine and shouted, "Sam, you must come home! Mother wants you. Right away. Father fell off the hay wagon, while they were piling hay. He fell off the *top* of the wagon. Come home with me, Sam. He's dying!"

The sandy rasp of the sleet grew louder against the pane, then faded as Slater drowsed asleep and began to dream.

He stood with Jedediah Strutt in the New Mill at Duffield. The old gentleman was telling him how a mob of angry Lancashire spinners had pushed their way into Mr. Arkwright's mill, in Chorley, a few years back, stoning the workers and smashing every carding machine and spinning frame in sight. Then Strutt was saying, "Samuel Slater, how'd ye like to be my overseer, at the New Mill, starting Monday week?" Slater read the date: July 22, 1789. The date his indenture would come to an end. The day on which his six-and-one-half year apprenticeship would be served out in full.

And right after that, he had read an advertisement in the *American Gazette*—a Philadelphia newspaper—saying that some Yankee would pay one hundred pounds to any Englishman who could help set up a first-rate Arkwright spinning mill over there.

Well, he had thought, if anyone's going to get that money it might as well be *you*, Sam Slater. And that was why he had commenced to stare so hard at the machines in the New Mill—at the whirring spindles, the notched and fluted rollers on the drawing frames, and the curved, clawlike teeth on the cylinders of the carding machines. How else could he ever hope to remember it all? He wouldn't even say goodbye to Mother, or to Mr. Strutt. He'd already served out his indenture, fair and square. He'd just take a few clothes, and the little money he'd saved, and he'd step off to London and find himself a ship and buy passage to America. He couldn't take any models or plans of the machines with him. Not out of England. For the King's customs officials would search him. If they found out that he'd worked in a spinning mill, they'd *never* let him leave the country. No. He'd say he was a farmer. He was big and ruddy. He *looked* like a plowboy. He'd sew up his indenture in the sleeve of his coat, and he'd sail.

Sixty-six days later, he'd be poking around Philadelphia, hunting a job. Then he'd move on to New York. And there he'd hear about a fellow named Moses Brown who owned a broken-down mill up around Providence, Rhode Island.

He'd sit down on December 2, 1789, and begin his letter to him, saying: "Sir—a few days ago I was informed that you wanted a manager of cotton spinning, etc., in which business I flatter myself that I can give the greatest satisfaction, in making good machinery, making good yarn, either for stockings or twist, as any that is made in England; as I have had opportunity, and an oversight of Sir Richard Arkwright's works, in Mr. Strutt's mill, upwards of six years. If you're not provided for, I should be glad to serve you. If you please to drop a line respecting the amount of encouragement you wish to give, you will much oblige, sir, your most obedient, humble servant, Samuel Slater."

He turned on his pillow and again heard the rasp of icy pellets on the windowpanes. He was half awake. Something had worried him, in the dream. He had stood before the main cylinder of Mr. Strutt's breaker, and he'd studied the teeth. The teeth were curved forward in the direction in which the cylinder turned . . .

But that was it! The teeth were *curved!* He sat up in bed and beat the mattress with his hand.

"That's what you forgot, Sam Slater!" he said, punching the mattress again with his fists. His heart was thumping with excitement. "The teeth on the main cylinder must all be *curved,* you idiot! The teeth must all be *curved!*"

# CHAPTER SEVEN

# Two Thousand Pounds of Yarn

When all the Wilkinsons were seated at the breakfast table next morning, Samuel Slater sat with bowed head until Father Oziel had finished saying grace. Then he smiled.

"Mother and Father Wilkinson, I have some good news," he said quietly. "I think I know what's wrong with my breaker! I went to bed last night troubled as I could be. The parts of all those machines of mine seemed to be spinning around in my brain—like the wheels in the prophet Ezekiel's vision. I dreamed I was a boy, back in Duffield, in Mr. Strutt's old mill."

"Samuel, thou didst not," said Hannah.

"I did. And I stood in front of my old breaker again, and stared at the teeth on the main cylinder. And then and there I saw what it was that went wrong yesterday!"

"Somethin' wrong with the teeth?" cried Smith Wilkinson, jumping up from the table.

"Something *terrible* wrong with the teeth, Master Wilkinson," said Samuel Slater, with a laugh. "The teeth on my cylinder set straight out, and the leather backing that holds them on the drum is too soft. So they slip, and give, when the cylinder turns. But Mr. Strutt's machine had teeth set in stiff cowhide, and even *more* important, the teeth on his machine were *curved!* Curved, like claws, to grip the cotton lap to the cylinder."

"By the all-merciful Providence!" roared Oziel Wilkinson. "They got to be curved!"

"Is *that* all that's wrong?" asked Lydia Wilkinson. "Why, Samuel, thou shalt have thy machine in first-rate runnin' order this very day, if *that's* all that's wrong with it!"

"Oh, Samuel!" said Hannah, springing up from her place and throwing her arms around his neck. Then she gave him a kiss on the cheek.

"Hannah!" said Oziel Wilkinson, beginning to bristle with anger. "I'll pack thee off to the Friends' School in Providence if . . ."

"Father Wilkinson," said Samuel Slater. "I beg you to—to give me your daughter Hannah in marriage. Don't say no, Father. I am not a Friend, I know. But I love Hannah, and . . ."

"And I love Mr. Slater," said Hannah.

"Wherever you may send her, Father," said Samuel Slater, "I shall follow her. Even to the ends of the earth."

Oziel's face grew red, and he opened his mouth to speak.

"Oziel Wilkinson," said his wife, "be thou silent, and consider well thy next words before speakin'."

"Oh, Ma!" said Hannah, bursting into tears.

Oziel closed his mouth, and heaved a long sigh.

"Let's find Pliny Earl and set us to work, curvin' them teeth," said Oziel Wilkinson. "Weddin's can wait. But we hev a loft full of raw cotton to spin, ain't we, Samuel?"

"I'll run get Mr. Earl," said Smith Wilkinson, and he rushed out into the snow and was gone.

Samuel Slater and Oziel and Daniel and Abraham strode over to the mill. Slater picked up some pieces of a broken grindstone in the mill yard and hurried up the ladder to the second floor. He and Oziel and Abe and Daniel were beating the teeth with the broken bits of grindstone when Pliny Earl and Smith Wilkinson and Sylvanus Brown came panting up the ladder to the breaker machine. They all began hammering away with the bits of the grindstone, curving the teeth so that they bent toward the doffing cylinder. Bent in that manner, they should hold the cotton blanket firmly to the main cylinder as the fibers passed through the fixed combs at the top of the drum.

"Abe and I best take the broken gear over to the forge," said Oziel. "We got to copy it real careful. And about that other matter. The weddin'. I calculate I'm willin', Samuel, if Hannah is."

In less than two hours, the two Wilkinson men were back at the breaker with a new gear. And Samuel Slater had just one more band of teeth to bend and hammer into shape on the main cylinder. By the time the machine was ready to be tested again, everyone who had been there the day before had heard the good news and had come hurrying back to the mill.

Even Moses Brown was on hand, for his sleigh had come hissing through the snowy ruts while the last of the pounding and hammering was still echoing from the second story.

"Friend Slater," he panted, from the top of the ladder, "hast thou lost thy senses? Wouldst thou smash thy costly machinery to bits? I heard of thy disappointment yesterday, and am come in haste to bid thee take courage."

"Nay, Moses Brown," laughed Oziel Wilkinson, "we ain't *smashin'* thy contraptions! Samuel Slater hez hed a vision, in a dream, more wonderful than that of the prophet Ezekiel! And he hath accordingly *curved* the teeth on his breaker. And now thou shalt see thy loft *full* of cotton, spun into gold, by his spinnin' machines!"

"Ready with the flywheel, Sam Jenks?" asked Samuel Slater.

"Ready, Mr. Slater," said Sam.

"Ready at the breaker belt, Smith Wilkinson?"

"Ready, Brother Slater," said Smith Wilkinson, with a grin.

Sam Jenks threw the lever and engaged the water wheel. Again the breaker shuddered. Her rollers purred and whirred and turned. The cotton was again spread deftly on the breaker belt. Smith Wilkinson's left hand darted time after time into the hamper for more of the woolly fluff. The main cylinder picked up its white blanket and slowly began rotating it toward the teeth of the fixed combs at the top of the machine. As the cotton neared the immovable combs, Slater held his breath.

The curved teeth on the main cylinder held the cotton firmly in place. Gently, smoothly, the white blanket hissed through the teeth of the fixed combs, brushed like the soft and shining hair of a maiden. Still fixed to the main cylinder, the silky tide of cotton reached the doffer and was neatly caught by its teeth. Then the toothed plate deftly plucked the thin cotton blanket from the far side of the doffer cylinder, and an even lap of cotton—a smooth, flat, cottony ribbon of fibers—started moving out between the final pair of rollers and fell, in soft folds, into the waiting basket.

"It's perfect," said Slater. "A *perfect* lap of cotton. Ready for the finisher. I *told* you I could do it, Mr. Moses Brown. And it looks as if I *have!*"

The finisher took the wide lap of cotton, stretched it and combed it further, and delivered a fine, three-inch-wide sliver of cotton fiber that coiled itself into the waiting can.

When the slivers were fed into the drawing frame, they were stretched on more rollers. As they passed through the reed, they were separated into narrower slivers, which were further stretched and twisted on the roving frame.

The twisted slivers were rapidly rolled up onto bobbins, and when the full bobbins were carried downstairs to the spinning frame, Torpen and Eunise Arnold soon had the spindles of their water frame humming and whirring, twisting up fine, even cotton yarn.

Everywhere Moses Brown looked, machines were whirring and thumping. Fine, spidery cotton threads were whirling through rollers, twirling on spindles. As the din increased, the balls of yarn grew fatter and fatter.

John and Varnus and Jabez Jenks, Otis Borrows and Charles and Annie Torpen—all the children tending the machines—stood ready to slip into place behind the moving gears and rollers. For if a thread should break anywhere, they would have to dart in among the moving parts and quickly knot the broken ends together.

The click and chatter and swish and rumble of the machines made the floor of the mill tremble. The air was filled with a busy drone, like the humming in a hive of bees.

Twenty-four strands of cotton were whirling on the spindles of one of the frames. On the second, forty-eight more were twisting and spinning, all at one time.

Moses Brown stared numbly at the dancing, whirling filaments of cotton. The machines throbbed and sang, happily, as if they loved nothing better than to draw infinite num-

bers of geometric diagrams with endless skeins of white.

Hannah Wilkinson smiled at Samuel Slater. Then she shook her head at Moses Brown.

"Art thou not ashamed to have doubted my dear Samuel, Mr. Moses Brown?" said she. "Be thou ever so careful, lest he whirl away *everything* in the loft above, and leave thee with not *half* enough money to buy all the cotton his insatiable machines can swallow!"

"True. Very true, Mr. Brown," said Samuel Slater, with a grin. "By this time next year—if my machines run fair, and if my calculations are correct—I shall have spun you up *two thousand pounds* of yarn!"

"Two thousand pounds of yarn!" exclaimed Moses Brown, over the clack and whir of the frames. "Oh, my winsome Hannah! Oh, my dear Friend Slater! Can it be that *ever* I doubted thee? For a time, I tormented myself, and vexed thee, for fear thy machines might *never* start turnin'. But now, see how they hum! Hannah, how well thou hast expressed my present concern. For now I dread, Friend Slater, that unless thou shuttest down thy whirlin' bobbins and closest up thy gates, thou shalt spin up *all my farms* into spools of cotton yarn!"

# About This Story

Anyone interested in learning more about Samuel Slater and the growth of the textile industry will want to read three books to which I am chiefly indebted in writing this story. They are *Memoir of Samuel Slater*, by George S. White (Philadelphia, 1836); *Samuel Slater: Father of American Manufactures*, by E. H. Cameron (Portland, Maine, 1960); and *The Story of Textiles*, by Perry Walton (Boston, 1912).

Slater was called "The Father of American Manufactures" with good cause. Before he sailed to America in 1789, no spinning mill in the United States had been able to eliminate hand labor completely, throughout the many stages of yarn production. That Slater was able to do so, and to reproduce each of the necessary carding and spinning machines from *memory*, and to set them all in motion by means of waterpower, will never cease to be amazing. His achievement is a most significant event in American history, for Slater brought with him to Pawtucket nothing less than the beginnings of the Industrial Revolution.

The manufacture of cotton textiles was a key industry in the early years of that revolution (which was both glorious and dismal), and Samuel Slater (1768–1835) had an intimate knowledge of most of the inventions that were so very important in the spinning and weaving trades: John Kay's flying shuttle, 1733; James Watt's steam engine, 1769; Richard Arkwright's water-powered spinning frame, 1769; James Hargreaves' spinning jenny, 1770; Samuel Crompton's "mule," 1779; and Edmund Cartwright's power loom, 1785. (It is interesting to note that in 1790, when this story takes place, three more years would have to pass before Eli Whitney would patent his cotton gin, whose invention completed the sequence of events that made the growing, spinning, and weaving of cotton one of the principal industries in the western world.) When Slater set his machines running in Rhode Island, America was taking her first step into the world of modern manufacturing.

Slater's machines were soon copied, and rival water-powered spinning mills began to spring up in many of the river towns of New England. They were followed by the growth of mill towns in other parts of the country, wherever there were streams powerful enough to turn machinery.

As the Industrial Revolution spread, it brought skilled workers to America from British mill towns. It gave employment to the poor, and produced lower prices and more plentiful goods for consumers. But its bright promises of ease and abundance were closely followed by gathering shadows. For the Industrial Revolution *also* gave rise to suffering, and to social upheavals and antagonisms which are still unresolved. It gave impetus to the polarization of labor and capital, to the growth of cities and of labor unions, to the spread of air and water pollution, to crowding in miserable slums, and to the cruelties of child labor. And these are only the most obvious of the huge problems that engulfed England, America, and other parts of the world in the wake of the machine age.

The increase in production and the initial lowering of prices (which Samuel Slater and the tribe of manufacturers who followed after him first presented to us) have proved to be mixed blessings indeed. The world will surely be dealing for the rest of this century with problems that arose because of the Industrial Revolution. Some of these problems may never be solved.

But I did not tell this story in order to suggest that we should blame Moses Brown and Samuel Slater for the evils that followed upon the factory system—evils which they could not possibly have foreseen. I told it because I was fascinated with Slater's shrewd grasp of the opportunities for success awaiting him in America, and because I marvel at his mnemonic feat. And I was charmed by canny Moses Brown's delightful blend of business acumen and benevolence, which had also been—on a larger scale—qualities that delighted us in Benjamin Franklin.

For those who, like me, like to know What Happened Next, I shall add that Moses Brown (1738–1836) lived another forty-six years, dying at ninety-eight. A prosperous merchant and manufacturer, he was also a good Quaker and helped found the Rhode Island Abolition Society. The year before he died, he was sought out and interviewed as to his opinions on emancipation by the young abolitionist William Lloyd Garrison, who would later found the influ-

ential abolitionist newspaper *The Liberator*. And Moses
and his wealthy nephew Nicholas Brown both left large
endowments to Rhode Island College—later named Brown
University after these benefactors.

Samuel Slater married his beloved Hannah Wilkinson on
October 2, 1791, and fathered a large family of children—
seven sons and two daughters. He never returned to England to visit his old home, though he sent some of the first
yarn spun on his machines back to his former master, Jedediah Strutt, to show him how good it was. Strutt said that
if he had had any idea how good a businessman Slater
would become, he would *never* have let him leave England,
at any price!

After Slater's death, his son William—named after Samuel's father—returned to England and bought "Holly
House," the old family farm.

Samuel Slater's success in America was almost instan-
taneous. Moses Brown wrote of it in 1791 to Alexander
Hamilton, and in his famous *Report on Manufactures*, our
first Secretary of the Treasury referred to Slater's recent
achievement in setting up the first water-powered spinning
frames in the young United States.

Slater grew very rich indeed, founded several more mills,
and in 1827 built, in Providence, the first spinning frames
and power looms in America to be run by steam. By the
time of his death, he was recognized throughout the United
States as the leading manufacturer of his age.

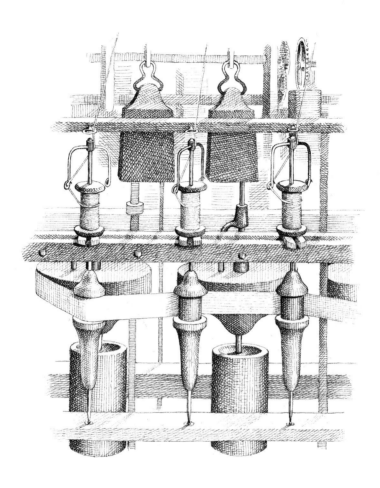